The Elements of
Expressive
Conducting

Choral Excerpt
Supplement

The Elements of
Expressive
Conducting
Michael Haithcock

Choral Excerpt
Supplement
Carole Ott Coelho

Brian K. Doyle

Kevin M. Geraldi

Conway Publications
Tecumseh, MI
2021

Conway Publications publishes works that further
the publisher's objective of excellence
in music, music education and research.

Conway Publications, Tecumseh, MI
Copyright © 2021 by Conway Publications
www.Conway-Publications.com

Library of Congress Cataloging-in-Publication Data
Haithcock, Michael
with Carole Ott Coelho, Brian K. Doyle, Kevin M. Geraldi
The Elements of Expressive Conducting / Michael Haithcock
Choral Excerpt Supplement /
Carole Ott Coelho, Brian K. Doyle, Kevin M. Geraldi
ISBN: 978-1-7332287-6-3
1. Music – Music Education.   2. Conducting
I. Haithcock, Michael   II. The Elements of Expressive Conducting
III. Choral Excerpt Supplement
Library of Congress Control Number: 2021939003

Cover art by
Tom Hodgman

CP 00100309

Conway
Publications

Printed in the United States of America
on acid-free paper

Table of Contents

Note: The music excerpts for chapters 1-13 are self-contained in *The Elements of Expressive Conducting*. Choral excerpts are provided beginning with Chapter 14.

Chapter 14: Beat Patterns as an Expressive Element

Chapter 15: Shaping Beat Patterns to Musical Expectation

Chapter 16: Expressive Tools for Shaping Sound

Chapter 17: Expression Through Extended Meters

Chapter 22: Fermatas and Their Musical Requirements

About the Authors

Michael Haithcock assumed his duties as director of bands and professor of music (Conducting) at the University of Michigan in the fall of 2001 after twenty-three years on the faculty of Baylor University. Following in the footsteps of William D. Revelli and H. Robert Reynolds, Professor Haithcock conducts the internationally renowned University of Michigan Symphony Band, guides the acclaimed band and wind ensemble graduate conducting program, and provides administrative leadership for all aspects of the University of Michigan's diverse and historic band program. In February of 2012, he was named an Arthur F. Thurnau Professor by the University of Michigan which is the University's highest award for excellence in undergraduate teaching. A graduate of East Carolina University, where he received the 1996 Outstanding Alumni Award from the School of Music, and Baylor University, Haithcock has done additional study at a variety of conducting workshops including the Herbert Blomstedt Orchestral Conducting Institute. He is in constant demand as a guest conductor with professional ensembles, major universities, all-state, and festival ensembles. He is also a resource person for conducting symposiums and workshops in a variety of instructional settings including Carnegie Hall's Weill Institute.

Ensembles under Haithcock's guidance have received a wide array of critical acclaim for their high artistic standards of performance and repertoire. These accolades have come through concert reviews at national and state conventions, performances in major concert venues such as Carnegie Hall in New York City, Walt Disney Concert Hall in Los Angeles, and a variety of performances presented during the Symphony Band's May 2011 tour of China, as well as recordings on the Albany, Arsis, and Equilibrium labels. A recent review of Symphony Band recordings in *Winds Magazine* proclaimed: "programming and execution of this caliber ought to be available worldwide...musically impressive, giving a sense of elation" while the American Record Guide praised the "professional manner with which the group delivers...they show great skill and artistry" and proclaimed the "sound of the UM Symphony Band is something to savor."

Professor Haithcock is an elected member of both the music honor society Pi Kappa Lambda and the American Bandmasters Association. He remains active in the College Band Directors National Association following his term as president of the organization (2001–2003). In 2011, he was awarded the Distinguished Service to Music Medal by Kappa Kappa Psi National Honorary Band Fraternity.

Carole Ott Coelho is Associate Director of Choral Activities at the University of North Carolina at Greensboro. Her degrees include the Master of Music and Doctor of Musical Arts in conducting from the University of Michigan where she studied with Jerry Blackstone and Theo Morrison. She also holds a Bachelor of Music in Music Education from the University of Cincinnati College-Conservatory of Music where her primary instrument was French Horn. While pursuing graduate studies at the University of Michigan, Dr. Ott received a double Grammy Award for her role in the preparation of William Bolcom's *The Songs of Innocence and of Experience*.

At UNCG, Dr. Ott directs the University Chorale, teaches undergraduate and graduate conducting, and free improvisation. Dr. Ott frequently appears as a clinician and guest conductor both regionally and nationally and is a recipient of The American Prize in Choral Conducting. An active soprano, Dr. Ott has appeared with the New Baroque Chamber Players and is a member of Anima Vox, a flute and soprano duo specializing in seamless concert experiences and free improvisation. Recent research interests include free improvisation in the traditional concert setting, vocal chamber music, and the music of José Joaquim Emerico Lobo de Mesquita. In 2018, she was a Fulbright Scholar to Minas Gerais, Brazil, where she researched eighteenth-century sacred music and taught free improvisation.

Brian K. Doyle joined the Crane School of Music faculty as director of bands in 2006. He conducts the Crane Wind Ensemble and Symphonic Band, and also teaches courses in conducting. A graduate of Michigan State University, his principal teachers included John Whitwell, Joseph Lulloff and James Forger. Doyle later received the AMusD in wind conducting under the mentorship of Michael Haithcock at the University of Michigan.

Dr. Doyle's former teaching posts include faculty positions at Indiana University, UNC-Chapel Hill, Duke University, and as a grade 5-12 public school music educator in Imlay City, MI. While in North Carolina, he served as the resident conductor of the Triangle British Brass Band and performed regularly as saxophonist with the North Carolina Symphony Orchestra. For ten summers, Dr. Doyle conducted ensembles at the renowned Interlochen Arts Camp. His summers are now spent conducting the Crane Youth Music Wind Ensemble. He is in regular demand as a clinician and conductor.

An elected member of American Bandmasters Association and an active member of the College Band Directors National Association, Dr. Doyle has served on the CBDNA Music Education Committee since 2013.

Kevin M. Geraldi is director of instrumental ensembles at the University of North Carolina at Greensboro, where he has served on the faculty since 2005. At UNCG, Dr. Geraldi conducts the Symphony Orchestra, Wind Ensemble, and Casella Sinfonietta, and teaches graduate and undergraduate conducting. Previously, he taught at Lander University in South Carolina and in the public schools of Westchester, IL.

Dr. Geraldi holds the Doctor of Musical Arts and Master of Music degrees in conducting from the University of Michigan, where he studied with Michael Haithcock and H. Robert Reynolds, and the Bachelor of Music Education degree from Illinois Wesleyan University, where he studied with Steven Eggleston. Additionally, he has studied and participated in workshops with teachers including Pierre Boulez, Frederick Fennell, Kenneth Kiesler, and Gustav Meier.

Maintaining an active schedule as a guest conductor, clinician and adjudicator, he also presents frequently at music education conferences throughout the country. His articles have been published by *The Instrumentalist*, the *Music Educators Journal*, *The Journal of Band Research* and the *WASBE Journal*. Dr. Geraldi is a recipient of the Conductors Guild's Thelma A.

Robinson Award and the UNCG School of Music Outstanding Teaching Award. He is an active member of the American Bandmasters Association, the College Orchestra Directors Association, the College Band Directors National Association, and the National Association for Music Education.

Foreword
by Michael Haithcock

This book contains musical excerpts designed to supplement those in the foundational textbook *The Elements of Expressive Conducting*. These carefully chosen materials offer educational opportunities to the emerging choral conductor that directly connect with their aspirations in the choral art. The authors are pleased to provide these additional examples in keeping with the student-centered values of Conway Publications. We are deeply indebted to Colleen Conway and Tom Hodgman for their ongoing support of our pedagogical mission.

These score examples have been chosen for their rich musical substance and pedagogical value, similar to those found in Appendix 2 of the primary text. Beginning with Chapter 14, each excerpt is carefully placed to align with and enhance the conducting principles developed sequentially throughout *The Elements of Expressive Conducting*. Thoughtful consideration has been given to the historical context of each excerpt and the diversity of the composers, while keeping the pedagogical considerations as the main objective.

Brian Doyle, Kevin Geraldi, and I welcome Carole Ott Coelho to our team of authors. Carole's expertise inspired this collection, as her familiarity with the pedagogy and deep knowledge of the choral repertoire was a significant component in curating the contents. My three colleagues have done all the difficult work of selecting and transforming the most meaningful materials possible for publication. As always, they have my profound gratitude for sharing their experience and insights in so many compelling ways.

The pedagogical principles scaffolded within *The Elements of Expressive Conducting* are universal to the philosophy of conducting with maximum expressive capacity. All who study the excerpts found in this supplement will deepen their understanding of this invaluable concept.

Michael Haithcock
Director of Bands
Arthur F. Thurnau Professor of Music
University of Michigan

Preface
by Carole Ott Coelho

I first experienced the pedagogy presented in *The Elements of Expressive Conducting* as a doctoral student in choral conducting at the University of Michigan, when I participated in the wind conducting seminar and studied with Michael Haithcock. The skills I learned during that semester blended beautifully with my training as a choral conductor. These studies expanded my understanding of conducting as a series of gestures grounded in my internalization of the score and emanating from natural movements of the body to communicate highly specific musical information to an ensemble. I am thrilled to join this team of authors and believe that the pedagogy of the foundational text and the collection of excerpts presented here will be transformational for both beginning and advanced choral conducting students.

I began to use this pedagogy with beginning choral conducting students several years ago when *The Elements of Expressive Conducting* was in draft form. Until then, I had built my class and syllabus using materials, repertoire, and knowledge from my experience. When I began using the text, the specifically sequenced concepts and the emphasis on natural movements of the body to express musical ideas elicited an incredible response from my students. They became more aware of themselves not only as conductors, but as musicians and artists. By moving through this pedagogy, my students began to understand the true nature of conducting – compelling musical leadership lead by a prepared mind and trained body – rather than a simple metrical representation of the music by a series of beat patterns. I was overjoyed when I learned that the book would be published by Conway Publications and available to the wider choral community.

The use of familiar songs in the foundational text, particularly "Twinkle Twinkle Little Star," gives choral students well known material with which to explore new movement concepts and allows them to immediately feel the effects of their gesture on a group of musicians. By delaying the introduction of beat patterns until Chapter 14, students are able to gain firm footing in body awareness concepts and the building blocks of expressive movement for conductors. Simple songs, such as "Mary Had a Little Lamb," allow students to create their own arrangements of music they know well while exploring new movement concepts and the cycle of stimulus and response in Units 1 and 2.

This supplement provides choral conducting students with carefully chosen choral score excerpts aligned with *The Elements of Expressive Conducting* beginning with Chapter 14. These selections offer opportunities to focus on refining skills in shaping sound, explore extended and mixed meters, subdividing, syncopation, cueing, and fermatas. Each chapter includes at least one excerpt in English as well as opportunities to explore French, German, Italian, Latin, Portuguese, and Spanish. In choosing these excerpts, we intentionally selected the highest quality musical examples by an inclusive list of composers. The set of excerpts aligned with each progressive chapter provides scaffolded musical challenges and music ranging from Mozart to Afro-Brazilian composer José Mauricio Nunes Garcia. Genres include traditional folk songs, part-songs, motets, a spiritual setting by H.T. Burleigh, and selections from larger choral-orchestral works. These works can be found in their entirety in public domain resources such as IMSLP and CPDL. Piano accompaniments range from simple reinforcement of vocal lines to orchestral reductions.

During the semester before publication of this supplement, I was able to explore many of the excerpts with my conducting students in detail. Some of the students tended toward music with which they were familiar, while others branched out into new sounds. By allowing students choice of repertoire, I found a heightened commitment in them to study, internalize, and step into the vulnerability necessary to truly express the music. A brief glance through the table of contents will reveal the depth and diversity of material available for exploration.

Chapter 14 begins with traditional folk songs and a sacred anthem composed by Samuel Coleridge-Taylor which introduces some simple expressive gestures. While working through Chapter 15, students can choose Mozart's familiar *Ave Verum Corpus*, or explore the less familiar *Rest Hath Come* by Florence Ashton Marshall. Students can experience the lush and expressive *My Lord What a Morning* set by H.T. Burleigh in Chapter 16 or expand their expressive skills with the sweet Spanish lullaby *Pajarito que cantas*. Gustav Holst's *Choral Hymns from the Rig Veda* underpins Chapter 17 as an exploration of extended meters. Excerpts from Mozart's *Missa Brevis in F Major* can be found in both Chapter 18 and Chapter 19 to develop skills in various types of subdivision. The lovely *Gondoliera* by Clara Schumann, in addition to selections from Handel and Haydn, helps students focus on preparations and syncopations Chapter 20. In Chapter 21, Nathaniel Dett's *Listen to the Lambs* offers a fantastic opportunity to introduce cueing in a fairly straightforward and sectional manner, while the *Beata Virgo* by Luís Álvarez Pinto scaffolds this skill by requiring cues in imitative stretto. Finally, Mendelssohn's *Cast thy burden upon the Lord from Elijah* is an excellent opportunity to work through fermatas at a fairly slow tempo in Chapter 22, while the Vivaldi *Suscepit Israel* involves both fermatas and tempo changes.

Many teachers of conducting spend considerable time and effort searching for pedagogically appropriate examples for conducting students from public domain resources and choral libraries. The 54 score excerpts presented here, along with the numerous excerpts found in *The Elements of Expressive Conducting,* provide teachers and students with a thorough pedagogical and philosophical understanding of conducting and the diverse materials necessary to hone their craft. I feel certain that the transformational nature of the material presented in both sources will allow students at any level to experience compelling musical leadership and the very nature of expressive conducting, transforming their gesture into the most authentic representation of the music and themselves.

Carole Ott Coelho
Associate Director of Choral Activities
University of North Carolina at Greensboro

14.1 Ludwig van Beethoven – Hymn to Joy

Friedrich Schiller   (1824)

1

14.2 Samuel Coleridge-Taylor – O ye that love the Lord

Psalm 97:10

14.3 Traditional – Coventry Carol

The Pageant of the Shearmen and Tailors

Lul - ly Lu - lay Thou li-ttle ti - ny child, Bye, bye lul - ly lu - lay.

1.O sis - ters too, how may we do, for to pre - serve this day; this
2.He - rod the king, in his rag - ing, set forth up - on this day; By
3.Then woe is me, poor child, for thee, And ev - er mourn and say; for

poor young - ling, for whom we sing, bye, bye, lul - ly lul - lay.
his de - cree, no life spare thee, bye, bye, lul - ly lul - lay.
thy par - ing, nor say nor sing, bye, bye, lul - ly lul - lay.

14.4 Traditional – Early One Morning

English folk-song

Early one morn-ing, just as the sun was ri-sing, I heard a maid sing in the val-ley be-low;

"Oh, don't de-ceive me! Oh, nev-er leave me! How could you use a— poor maid-en so?"

14.5 Traditional – My Country 'tis of Thee

Samuel Francis Smith (1831)

15.1 Johanna Kinkel – Ritters Abschied

Weh dass wir schei - den müs - sen Lass mich noch ein - mal küs - sen, Ich muss an Kai - ser's

Sei - ten in's fal - sche Welsch - land rei - ten. Fahr - wohl, fahr - wohl mein

ar - mes Lieb. Fahr - wohl, fahr - wohl___ mein ar - mes Lieb.

15.2 Samuel Coleridge-Taylor – Summer is gone

Christina Rossetti

Samuel Coleridge-Taylor – Summer is gone (p. 2)

15.3 Orlando di Lasso – Matona mia cara

Libro de Villanelle, Moresche, et altre Canzoni

(1581)

Orlando di Lasso – Matona mia cara (p.2)

15.4 Florence Ashton Marshall – Rest Hath Come

Leyland Leigh

(1883)

Florence Ashton Marshall – Rest Hath Come (p.2)

15.5 Wolfgang Amadeus Mozart – Ave Verum Corpus

K. 618
(1791)

Wolfgang Amadeus Mozart – Ave Verum Corpus (p.2)

15.6 Josquin des Prez – Mille Regrets

16.1 Traditional – Pajarito que cantas

16.2 Henry Purcell – I will give thanks unto Thee, O Lord

Psalm 138:1-8

Z. 20
(1684)

Henry Purcell – I will give thanks unto Thee, O Lord (p.2)

16.3 Johannes Brahms – "Wie lieblich sind deine Wohnungen"

Psalm 84:1,2,4

Ein deutches Requiem, op. 45
(1868)

Johannes Brahms – "Wie lieblich sind deine Wohnungen" (p.2)

16.4 José Mauricio Nunes Garcia – Ave Maris Stella

José Mauricio Nunes Garcia – Ave Maris Stella (p.2)

16.5 Gustav Holst – Swansea Town

Collected by George Gardiner

Six Choral Folksongs, op. 36b, H. 136

Allegro moderato

Gustav Holst – Swansea Town (p.2)

16.6 Harry Thacker Burleigh – My Lord, What a Morning

Revelations 8:10

Harry Thacker Burleigh – My Lord, What a Morning (p.2)

17.1 Franz Schubert – "Agnus Dei" from *Deutsche Messe*

D. 872
(1827)

Mein Hei - land, Herr und Meis - ter! Dein Mund so se - gens - reich, sprach einst das Wort des

Hei - les: "Der Frie - de sei mit Euch!" O Lamm, das op - fernd tilg - te der Mensch - heit schwere

Shuld,___ send' uns auch dei - nen Frie - den durch Dei - ne Gnad' und Huld.___

17.2 Percy Grainger – Horkstow Grange

Based upon a version sung by George Gouldthorpe
Goxhill, North Lincolnshire (1906/1908)

Percy Grainger – Horkstow Grange (p.2)

17.3 Gustav Holst – "Battle Hymn" from *Choral Hymns from Rig Veda*

Group 1, op. 26, H. 97
(1908)

Gustav Holst – "Battle Hymn" from *Choral Hymns from Rig Veda* (p.2)

17.4 Gustav Holst – "Funeral Hymn" from *Choral Hymns from Rig Veda*

Group 1, op. 26, H.97
(1908)

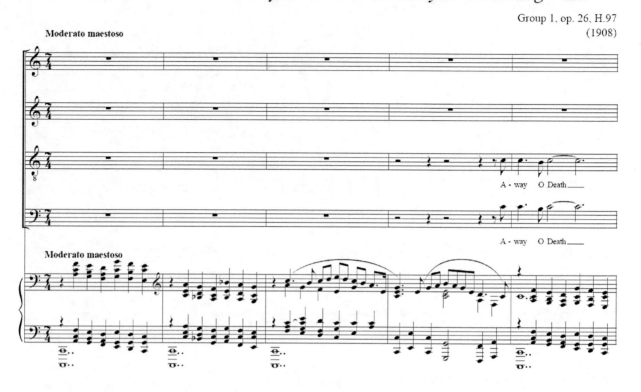

Gustav Holst – "Funeral Hymn" from *Choral Hymns from Rig Veda* (p.2)

17.5 Joseph Gabriel Rheinberger – "Eja Mater" from *Stabat mater*

op. 138
(1884)

Joseph Gabriel Rheinberger – "Eja Mater" from *Stabat mater* (p.2)

18.1 Gustav Holst – Lullay My Liking

Sloan Manuscript (15th c.)

op. 34, no. 2, H. 129

18.2 Herbert Howells – Here is the Little Door

Francis Chesterton

Herbert Howells – Here is the Little Door (p.2)

18.3 Wolfgang Amadeus Mozart – "Agnus Dei" from *Missa brevis in F major*

Wolfgang Amadeus Mozart – "Agnus Dei" from *Missa brevis in F major* (p.2)

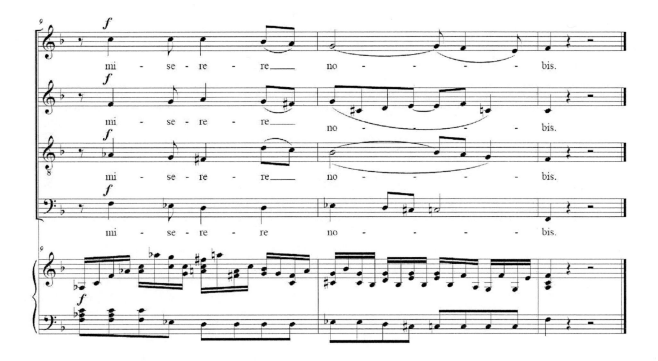

19.1 Samuel Coleridge-Taylor – The Lee Shore

19.2 Herbert Howells – A Spotless Rose

Catherine Winkworth (after *Es ist ein Ros entsprungen*)

With easeful movement

A Spot-less Rose____ is blow ing, Sprung from a ten - der root,____ Of

A Spot-less Rose is____ blow ing, Sprung from a ten - der root, Of

A Spot-less Rose____ is blow - ing, Sprung from a ten - der root,____ Of

A Spot-less Rose____ is blow - ing, Sprung from a ten - der root,____ Of

an-cient seers'____ fore-show-ing, Of Jes - se pro - mised fuit:____ Its fair-est bud____ un-

an-cient seers'____ fore-show-ing, Of Jes - se pro - mised fuit:____ Its fair-est bud____ un-

an-cient seers'____ fore-show-ing, Of Jes - se pro - mised fuit:____ Its fair-est bud____ un-

an-cient seers'____ fore-show-ing, Of Jes - se pro - mised fuit;____ Its fair-est bud____ un-

46

Herbert Howells – A Spotless Rose (p.2)

19.3 W. A. Mozart – "Dona nobis pacem" from *Missa brevis in F major*

W. A. Mozart – "Dona nobis pacem" from *Missa brevis in F major* (p.2)

19.4 Percy Grainger – Rufford Park Poachers

Based upon the version sung by Mr. Joseph Taylor
At Brigg, Lincolnshire, 4 August 1906

Percy Grainger – Rufford Park Poachers (p.2)

19.5 Traditional – A Lua Girou

arr. Ana Yara Campos

Traditional – A Lua Girou (p.2)

IPA guide – A lua girou

A lua girou, girou
[a lua ʒirow ʒirow]

traçou no céu um compasso
[traʃow nu sew ũ cõpasu]

Eu também quero fazer
[ew tãbẽ kɛru fazɛr]

um travesseiro dos teus braços
[ũ travɛsɐ̃jru dos teus brasus]

19.6 Peter Warlock – As Dew in Aprylle

Anonymous 15th Century

(1924)

Peter Warlock – As Dew in Aprylle (p.2)

19.7 Anonymous – Riu, Riu, Chiu

Villancicos de diversos Autores
(1556)

19.8 Claude Le Jeune – Revecy venir du Printans

Rechant à cinq

Re - ve - cy   ve - nir   du   Prin - tans   L'a-mou-reuz'   et   bel - le   sai - zon.

Re - ve - cy   ve - nir   du   Prin - tans   L'a-mou-reuz'   et   bel - le   sai - zon.

Re - ve - cy   ve - nir   du   Prin - tans   L'a-mou-reuz'   et   bel - le   sai - zon.

Re - ve - cy   ve - nir   du - Prin - tans   L'a-mou - reuz'   et   bel - le   sai - zon.

Re - ve - cy   ve - nir   du   Prin - tans   L'a-mou-reuz'   et   bel - le   sai - zon.

19.9 J. Rosamond Johnson – Lift Ev'ry Voice and Sing

James Weldon Johnson

20.1 Juana Inés de la Cruz – Madre, la de los primores

(1686)

20.2 Georg Frideric Handel – "Hallelujah Chorus" from *Messiah*

HWV 56

(1741)

Georg Frideric Handel – "Hallelujah Chorus" from *Messiah* (p.2)

20.3 Franz Joseph Haydn – "Awake the Harp" from *The Creation*

Hob. XXI: 2
(1798)

20.4 Henry Purcell – In These Delightful, Pleasant Groves

20.5 Florence Ashton Marshall – To Sea! The Calm is O'er

Thomas Lovell Beddoes

Florence Ashton Marshall – To Sea! The Calm is O'er (p.2)

20.6 Clara Schumann – Gondoliera

Emanuel Geibel

Clara Schumann – Gondoliera (p.2)

20.7 Antonio Vivaldi – "Fecit Potentiam" from *Magnificat*

RV 610
(1715)

Antonio Vivaldi – "Fecit Potentiam" from *Magnificat* (p.2)

20.8 Charles Villiers Stanford – The Blue Bird

Charles Villiers Stanford – The Blue Bird (p.2)

21.1 Edward Elgar – As Torrents in Summer

Henry Wadsworth Longfellow

(1896)

Edward Elgar – As Torrents in Summer (p.2)

21.2 Raphaella Aleotti – Miserere mei, Deus

Psalm 51

Raphaella Aleotti – Miserere mei, Deus (p.2)

21.3 Nathaniel Dett – Listen to the Lambs

Nathaniel Dett – Listen to the Lambs (p.2)

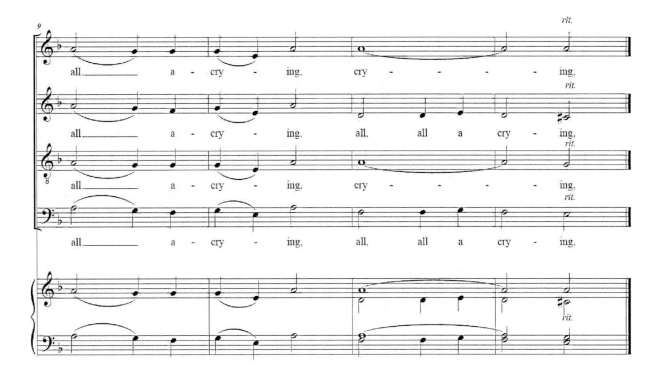

21.4 Edward Elgar – The Snow

Edward Elgar – The Snow (p.2)

21.5 Hans Leo Hassler – Cantate Domino

Psalm 95 [96]:1-3

Hans Leo Hassler – Cantate Domino (p.2)

21.6 Luís Álvares Pinto – Beata Virgo

Divertimento Harmónico no. 1
(1776)

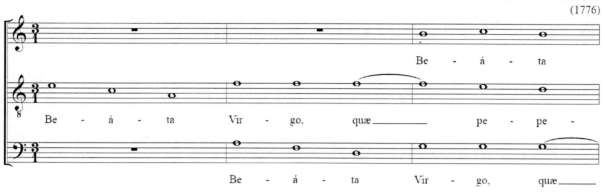

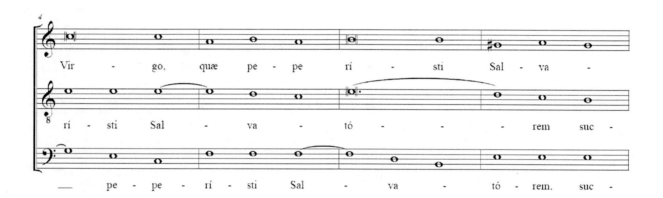

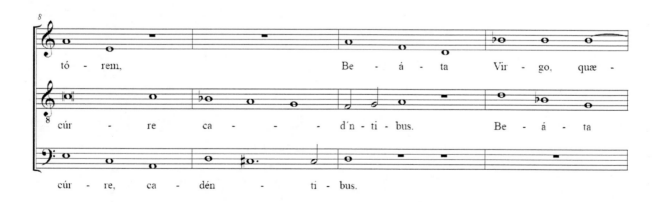

Luís Álvares Pinto – Beata Virgo (p.2)

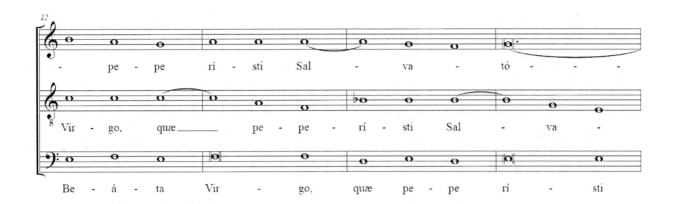

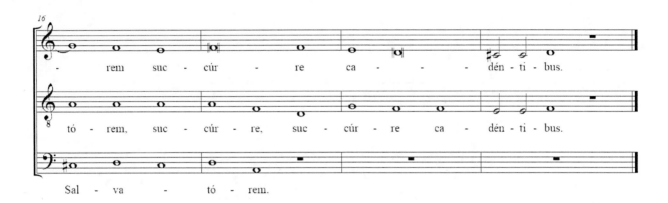

21.7 Thomas Tallis – If Ye Love Me

John 14:15-17

Thomas Tallis – If Ye Love Me (p.2)

22.1 Edward Elgar – My Love Dwelt in a Northern Land

Edward Elgar – My Love Dwelt in a Northern Land (p.2)

22.2 Franz Joseph Haydn – "In the beginning" from *The Creation*

Franz Joseph Haydn – "In the beginning" from *The Creation* (p.2)

22.3 Gustav Holst – I Love My Love ("Cornish Folksong")

Collected by George Barnet Gardiner

Six Choral Folksongs, op. 36. H. 136

Gustav Holst – I Love My Love ("Cornish Folksong") (p.2)

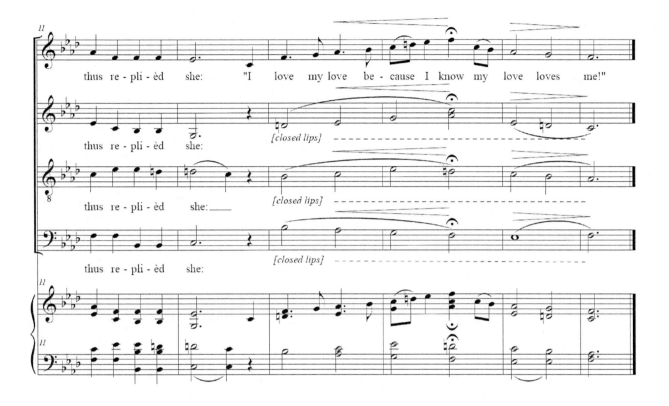

22.4 Felix Mendelssohn – "Cast thy burden upon the Lord" from *Elijah*

op. 70, MWV A 25

Felix Mendelssohn – "Cast thy burden upon the Lord" from *Elijah* (p.2)

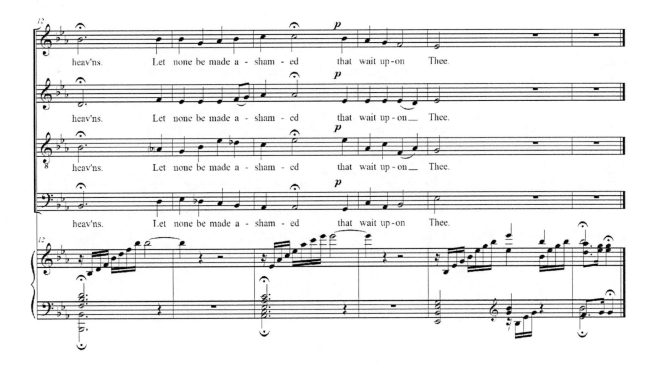

22.5 Antonio Vivaldi – "Suscepit Israel" from *Magnificat*

Antonio Vivaldi – "Suscepit Israel" from *Magnificat* (p.2)